SCRIBNER
POETRY

Also by Diana Khoi Nguyen

Ghost Of

Root Fractures

Poems

Diana Khoi Nguyen

SCRIBNER

NEW YORK   LONDON   TORONTO   SYDNEY   NEW DELHI

Scribner
An Imprint of Simon & Schuster, Inc.
1230 Avenue of the Americas
New York, NY 10020

First Scribner trade paperback edition January 2024

SCRIBNER and design are registered trademarks of The Gale Group, Inc.,
used under license by Simon & Schuster, Inc., the publisher of this work.

Simon & Schuster: Celebrating 100 Years of Publishing in 2024

For information about special discounts for bulk purchases, please contact Simon &
Schuster Special Sales at 1-866-506-1949 or business@simonandschuster.com.

The Simon & Schuster Speakers Bureau can bring authors to your live event.
For more information or to book an event, contact the Simon & Schuster
Speakers Bureau at 1-866-248-3049 or visit our website at www.simonspeakers.com.

Interior design by Kathryn A. Kenney-Peterson

Manufactured in the United States of America

10 9 8 7 6 5 4 3 2 1

Library of Congress Cataloging-in-Publication Data

Names: Nguyen, Diana Khoi, 1985– author.
Title: Root fractures : poems / Diana Khoi Nguyen.
Identifiers: LCCN 2023036027 (print) | LCCN 2023036028 (ebook) |
    ISBN 9781668031308 (paperback) | ISBN 9781668031315 (ebook)
Subjects: LCGFT: Poetry.
Classification: LCC PS3614.G85 R66 2024 (print) | LCC PS3614.G85 (ebook)
    | DDC 811/.6—dc23/eng/20230822
LC record available at https://lccn.loc.gov/2023036027
LC ebook record available at https://lccn.loc.gov/2023036028

ISBN 978-1-6680-3130-8
ISBN 978-1-6680-3131-5 (ebook)

Thank you to the editors of the following journals and publications in which these
poems, though sometimes in earlier versions or under different titles, originally
appeared: *New England Review*, *Chicago Review*, *Phi Kappa Phi*, *Texas Review*, *The
Journal*, Poets.org's *Poem-a-Day*, *Diacritics*, *Khora*, *Cordite Poetry Review*, *Kweli
Journal*, *Colorado Review*, and Belladonna*.

To my mother and father and their cha mẹ.

Table of Contents

Bài 7. Viết một đoạn văn về gia đình bạn.

Giờ đây, gia đình tôi là người Mỹ.

Chúng tôi có bốn, chứ không phải năm người.

Năm 1975 ba mẹ tôi là người Việt.

Họ là kỹ sư,

xây dựng cuộc sống mới ở đây

ở California, nơi họ gặp nhau.

Họ có ba người con,

hai gái một trai.

Con gái lớn là nhà văn,

con gái nhỏ làm trong bệnh viện.

Con trai đã chết.

Họ không sống cùng một nhà.

Có lẽ không lâu thôi họ sẽ là người Việt hay là xác chết.

Tất cả bọn họ rồi sẽ chết.

Cape Disappointment

in rising, articulation of the spine leaves one open for a slitting

daisies thread tread marks in the road

I cannot trace my body so press it against grass

from afar, I recognize the shivering seal pup on the trail

dreading blood on the beak pecking at a beached carcass, I stumble

Selkie Weaning Young

Finding her hide we trailed
                    fingers down then against
          grains of fur thrusting shoulders into its waxy skin.

                              This is how she found us
                the past draped about us like a cloak
hands twisting peach halves from a core.

                    Her form in the sound
a pandan leaf peeking through milk. The only seals in Vietnam:
                              American men with green faces.

Misinformation

Spring, a woman in suede pumps takes down every
        painting, revealing ghosts on the wall where frames used to hang.
Files rent in thin white strips, falling
               like ash, curl along embassy corridors.

                        A man adjusts his glasses
packs a satchel, the click of its buckle like a voice choking
      behind closed doors.
           He walks the same way home, gathering his family the way
an open palm sweeps stray grains of rice
                    into one corner of a kitchen table.

The Americans offer to take us with them, he says, though he doesn't know why.
                  His children do not know what he has seen.
      They wake and sleep to blooming bombs, whistling missiles.
                         War:
an instrument whose sound is absorbed and amplified in the body of a girl
      like mercury inside a fish.

          We are winning, my grandfather says. *The South will not lose this war.*

Đổi Mới

Months after he travels sixty miles after work with a coworker who insists they visit the family of a woman my father's never met, his girlfriend lying on the couch somewhere back where he had departed from, looking forward to their next night at the disco, my parents meet for the first time and my father learns that her father knew his father well. At the US embassy during the war, one served as a translator while one prepared copy. It has been only eight years since the last helicopter lifted from that roof, four years since my mother reunited with her family. On average, it takes four years to complete a baccalaureate, but the timeline for finding a husband is less clear. When the groom's family arrives at the bride's family home, they bear gifts of fruit and gold. Jewelry is exchanged between the parents and bride, husband and wife. After the wedding, my mother exchanges her rings for ones with clearer diamonds, rings I wouldn't accept unless they fit, and they did, after my parents dropped a bead of soap on my knuckle. Đổi Mới, or the launch of economic reform in Vietnam, just after I was born eight thousand miles away. Đổi Mới, meaning renewal more generally. At the time of their son's death, he joins my parents' fathers in the elsewhere. Daily life resumes after an interruption.

Notes on the Fractures

after Robert Hass

My seven-year-old mother climbs a ladder to retrieve a bottle of medicine for the soldier waiting at the counter whose face is covered in cystic acne, a white circle on the dusty shelf where the bottle had been. Each of them has a job they think they are good at.

I could say it is the moment just before "White Christmas" played over Armed Forces Radio. A sheet of newspaper tumbles in the street. A promissory note flies by. Two of my uncles are studying overseas, and neither sends word back about what's to come.

Light, pale white, white, fair, medium, yellow, yellow. Always check with a doctor beforehand. My mail carrier asks if I've had a baby because he's been delivering samples of formula to my door.

Upon returning to the trailhead, we tail a wedding shoot, our dogs scattered in the tall grass, the camera's flash like a globe in the field, mist rolling through cottonwood and lace. I think of their wedding day, where these photos would be framed beside a guest book.

After a frightening suicide threat, I get my brother to talk to someone and he goes on meds. His doctor tells me he's given her permission to share his files with me. The last time we spoke: "My libido is back," he reports. His last email, a year later: "Fuck off." Then: "i don't want therapy (more for you), i don't want medication (you could use some), and i don't want yours or anybody else's help. Oh and in case it doesn't seem obvious, there won't be anymore Skype 'meetings.' if you want though, feel free to find a gif of an Asian person nodding and smiling."

I could say that I was taught to nod and smile, listen and get along. Witnessing is a way of listening, and a way of catching what goes unsaid: a man takes his young sons, leaving his wife and daughters. They wake up in a country to a quiet they don't recognize, dust rising like smoke around bees, smoke without fire.

A Story About Holes

1.

A girl dug a hole at the beach, sent her siblings to fetch water.

She found pleasure in it. All things fall down, or want to,
so she dug and dug, her trowel falling deeper, the earth growing darker.

She thought in concentric circles, the tides coming
and going, overlapping each other. When she poured water in,
the hole filled up, then emptied, its walls caved in. She began again.
If she could have, she would have dug a hole every day, one
beside the other, then another, and another. A hole is a hole,
but none of them are the same.

Along a shore, no one can know how many holes there are.

Along a shore, no one can know which holes are hers.

2.

I typed my brother into a box. The search took 0.39 seconds and
there were as many entries as there were members of our family:
five, to be precise. Four if you don't count the one who didn't think
he was one of us.

From Latin *praecis*: "cut short."
From the verb *praecidere*, *prae-* "in advance" + *caedere* "to cut."

There is a hole inside the search box. A hole
and a frame, to delineate where things go in. The internet
doesn't know my brother died. Oliver Nguyen at MyLife.com®
Age: 27.

He cut his one-year-old self out of each frame. Three-, five-,
shy-of-two-, thirteen-year-old selves, too. Then at twenty-four,
out of the whole picture.

3.

Hard to say what could have happened.

—What happened?
—Happened?
—Yes.
—I didn't die.

All night the trees stand in lamplight. From out in the universe,
they are gliding about an axis. Staying still is a kind of moving.

Inside still ponderosa pines, silk-thin threads of water
sometimes break, exploding in small pops of music. A hole
in the air of their capillaries. A song of holes.

4.

I am a particle of the anti-past. A particle and its counterpart
quickly destroy each other. They blip into existence and then
they're out. The past and the anti-past multiply. 1 + 1 is 3.
As long as there are more particles than counterparts.

A history of particles: Once there were two particles; one
was a hole, the other had a stick. What came first, the hole
or the stick? I don't know, but soon there were more holes,
more sticks. Sticks found in holes, holes made by sticks.

Hawking showed that black holes can, like other holes, or sticks,
shrink and die. But there's a way out. Out of the black hole.

"If you feel you are in a black hole, don't give up—"

5.

This is a story about two particles. They are traveling near
an event horizon. Life at the edge can be peculiar. One
of the pair falls in with a negative valence
which sucks out energy from the black hole.

The other particle, its counterpart, escapes with positive energy.
No one knows how.

All night the pair stay silent in the dark, not touching.
The one who escapes informs us about the one who didn't.

This is a passing of their story from inside the black hole
to the outside. We used to think nothing ever came back out.

So here we are. One is here, the other one over there, but
we know what happened to him. That he exists.

Đổi Mới

Sometimes the skin's surface needs to break or be cut for healing to begin. The majority of antivenins are administered intravenously. That is, they take place within or inside a vein. Fang into flesh, needle through then under the skin. In a lab someone will seek to understand the biomechanics of spider fangs so as to inspire new medical devices. Into her body, my father's mother administers insulin. When examined up close, our pores make up a canvas for needlepoint. Health questionnaires do not ask if there is a history of violence in your family. To the question not asked, I want to ask, How many generations should I go back? When I dress exactly as my mother did on her honeymoon, is it not mimicry? One creature evolving to resemble another, in advantageous antipredator adaptation. But what if your predator also looks like you?

Đổi Mới

On an American billboard in 1975, two hands are cracking a white egg against a black backdrop, the yolk glistens mid-flight, identical in hue to the golden arches printed beside it.

Mid-flight, my father absently stares at his brother's leg, which may or may not contain a bullet wound.

Though he is sitting still, he is moving faster than he ever has before.

* * *

Back in his homeland, half of me exists inside an egg my mother hasn't yet expelled. Together, we are rounded up, moving north to a reeducation camp.

Where she will encounter gruel instead of cháo. Flies instead of rice.

* * *

The flies gather around her bowl like photojournalists racing to the execution of a Việt Cộng officer on the streets of Chợ Lớn.

* * *

Chợ Lớn, or "big market," is the largest Chinatown in the world.

Despite Việt Nam's persecution of the Chinese following a border war in 1979.

If you treat someone ill enough, they will ~~try to~~ leave.

* * *

Before this war, there was another war, and before that war, another war, yet another one, and another, et al.

War^n.

I say "et al." (which translates to "and others") instead of "et cetera" because there are many authors to a war, and the line of wars and their authors is too long to untangle here.

$War^{n^{author^n}}$.

* * *

To type a superscript, you have to press Control-Shift-Command-Plus Sign. The first three keys are clustered near one another.

War control shift command + War shift control command + War command shift control +

The order in which they occur doesn't matter; the result is the same: War^n.

* * *

The first time I heard "Việt Cộng" I actually heard "Việt con," which was exactly what I was, a Vietnamese child.

A child precedes and follows a war. We use different words for during.

Hostage, soldier, victim. Shooter, killer, Charlie. Body beside, body below, parts of the body.

* * *

Is it worse if the child goes unnoticed, dead or alive? Intact or in parts?

"In my country," my mother says, "a child shows love by listening to her parents without question."

But what if the parents are wrong?

* * *

Việt Cộng, Việt con, con viết. If I fail to use the right diacritics, I fail to say what I mean.

In Vietnamese, the meaning of a word depends on the tone of each vowel.

In order to remember the sounds of each tone, I rely on words that rhyme: viết, giết. Giết, viết.

Con biết giết không?

* * *

If I mispronounce or misspell, I end up with something else entirely.

Con vịt.

A duck will try to fly, even after decapitation. It flaps and flaps, unable to right a wrong.

* * *

In 1986, a country reopens market doors. But đổi mới happens every time something ends.

When an American diplomat invites your family to the airport on April 25, 1975. When you move out of your parents' Californian home and into your husband's.

If you give birth, not knowing that your son will take his own life twenty-four years later, is this life change a new one, or part of the longer chain which began once the war ended?

Actually, where is the beginning, that war? Or the one before it?

* * *

Đổi mới, *not* đời mới.

Đổi đời, so you must open yourself to it.

* * *

I lost my first tongue when my parents forbade me from using it. At first, it was an equitable exchange of borders: they spoke to me in Vietnamese, I replied in English.

Perhaps my parents thought they were building a mini colony in a suburban cul-de-sac. *Did you see that Asian family moving in?* my neighbors must've asked one another. A bright yolk enclosed in a white, smooth-pored egg.

It is through language that colonization quietly takes over one's imagination.

I thought the Vietnamese word for faucet was *robinet*.

* * *

For me, to be American is not to go back to Vietnam, but to fly there for the first time.

In Vietnam, they know immediately where I am from.

* * *

Vòi nước. I looked it up. "Tentacle (for) water," if you break down the phrase. My father's French Catholic school nudging him to wash his hands beneath the *robinet*.

"The nuns, they hit your left hand until you learn to write right-handed," he told me once.

* * *

With a cul-de-sac, you have to exit where you entered. But there's space to turn around.

A native egg exits the ovary, never turning back.

Inside the womb, a fetus will toss and turn frequently during pregnancy. My brother took his life in the garage, a place where he arrived the day my parents brought him home from the hospital nursery.

* * *

It may be best to decolonize my lost tongue before retrieving it. To do so, I need to rescind the tacit permission French took in entering my mouth.

I will spit it out, spit it out, spit it out.

But how to scrub the tentacle of imagination?

* * *

In my faucet there wages a war. Rages a war.

* * *

Decolonization is not as simple as closing a door. It begins by picking up where my four-year-old self left off.

What will happen when I can tell my story in my mother tongue?

Again

after Melisa Tien

A woman gives birth, and a new word gets added to a list of those that describe her.

"This, too, will befall her," she fears. But she has another daughter, then a son. Then she forgets about her daughters. At least that's what you think.

When the son dies, the family forgets themselves a bit more than they usually do, like a hole that expands only to contract shortly thereafter.

Again.

Because she could not forget the labor pains as she could not forget the country left behind, the mother decides one child is enough.

With her husband, she teaches the daughter that every thing has at least two names: water, nước. Nước, country. They encourage the daughter, as they would've encouraged all their children, had they had others.

"But you have to be practical," they tell their only child.

Again.

They tell her, "Remember Dr. Seuss; you are limited only by what you can imagine." Oh, the thinks you can think.

The daughter learns to swim, to start a fire (tepee and log cabin), to make tonkotsu. She fails at first, but gets back up. Fails, and gets back up. Each time she fails, she fails a little less, then finds new ways to fail.

The mother does not tell the daughter that this is how you transport yourself to a new ~~country~~ nước.

Again.

Every few years, the mother and daughter return to Vietnam, wandering down alleys until they eat their way back home.

"That would've been me," the daughter says, nodding at a woman picking up noodles. Soup for her child and her parents next door, she thinks.

The mother points at a figure striding into the temple, áo dài curling like incense. "No, that one is me," pointing instead at a woman on a motorbike balancing market greens and three children.

Amid the din of street traffic and sizzling meats, the faint sound of a drum, someone's hand testing tension on stretched buffalo skin.

And if the end of the war wasn't the end of anything, and the war was what it was: another plastic bead on a string of worthless beads.

She would have endured the lean years, finding herself married, a mẹ, then a bà ngoại, in Đổi Mới.

Every Friday she would eat ốc with her grandchildren at their favorite stall, and her cháu would show her what they made, gifts she stowed on the windowsill beside her bed.

Again.

She never marries, throws herself deeper into school, helping her mother with the secret pharmacy. When you are forced to disband, keep on going, just underground.

Again.

She marries later, after finishing school. In the lab, she meets her future husband, and when they welcome their first child, a son, he looks just like the daughter they didn't have.

She marries later, yes, says, "Perhaps we stop at one," after giving birth to their son. But the husband always wanted daughters, so a compromise, a tear which becomes a chasm begins.

Again.

A catch in the shower where all their long hairs tangle, slowing ~~water~~ nước down the drain.

A bandaged hand does nothing to soften a mother's blow. But you can strike with words, the child learns, striking to stop the blows received, not realizing how a shield also cuts.

No. Again.

Exasperated, the mother says something she shouldn't have.

Her daughter snaps back so fast the mother nearly flinches. Then silence, like a box of bullets, nestles in.

Two strong women, in their difficult hour.

The mother does not see or hear from her daughter for several years and it is as if—

A time comes when neither daughter nor mother should have to respond to one another anymore.

I was thinking of you, neither of them writes.

Oh, the thinks you can think.

Again.

The mother pops into her neighborhood library for the first time in years. Time, like a great distance, can make an alien of you.

She misses her children. Perhaps she sees them again, reading to each other, rifling through the picture books.

Again.

The mother doesn't have a daughter. The daughter, she doesn't have children of her own. When they meet by chance, as tourists at a boat show in Huế, they realize that they are both poets. What are the odds?

Drifting along the Perfume River, a boat peers into a mirror.

What's the difference between a mirror and a window? You see yourself in one, your ghost in the other.

Again.

A ghost can host (an)other. A mother.

Trong mọi thứ bạn là, bạn trong mọi thứ.

The daughter takes her own life, because it is a way of taking her mother's.

Again.

When the daughter miscarries, the mother flies over immediately. They sit on the daughter's bed, peeling and passing a pomelo between them.

That which leaves the body cannot reenter.

Again.

Out on the ice, the daughter jigs her line, hoping for a bite. Below, hundreds of fish thrash and bruise on their way to spawn. They will spawn and die, or die trying.

Only after she guts her catch does the kokanee yield its clutch of eggs. Something inside the daughter's body drops.

Why is time always running out?

"Hello," says the mother.

"Hi, Mama," says the daughter.

"Is everything okay?"

"Dą, just cleaning, and thought of you."

A voice, like a seam, can bridge a rupture.

But language fails, eventually.

In a memory from before, or one to come, the mother and the daughter walk the foam line of a beach at dusk. The evening fog which kisses one, kisses both.

Perhaps one is carrying a small child, or letting go an old ghost. Or one holds her mother's hand.

And the tide flowing and receding, inches further inland, like a palm erasing where they have been.

Đổi Mới

At the site where the wound will occur, we know that she was in the garden, the one she had cultivated, seed by seed, shortly after moving in with her husband and their eleven children, all of them together again after years of separation, her husband's and sons' feet in America, her daughters' and hers in Vietnam, first in Saigon, then a place unmentioned by the coast, underground, in hiding, waiting to make a successful bribe so they might board a vessel, any vessel: collective bride in dark waters facing an unknown stage. Bướm bướm, she whispered to my mother, butterfly, the word my mother used to reference our genitals, two cupped wings like a heartbeat, bướm bướm. In hiding all that year unmentioned by the coast, my mother as a young girl had her first period, its dark liquid unseen in their nest underground. Bướm bướm, the smear of red between my thighs perfectly symmetrical. Two lips pressed together as if to kiss, or to strike.

At the site where the wound will occur, there will be two tiny holes, the size of motes. When a spider bites, she thrusts fangs into her prey, fangs curved in order to hold the prey in place. In the case of megafauna such as bà ngoại, a black widow strikes because she is startled. Through the chin-height window above the kitchen sink I see her moving through the thick foliage of her compact garden, one hand directing water from a hose, the other moving in tandem to words I cannot hear but know from the movement of her lips. It is almost time for the avocados, she will tell me, and do I remember where this tree came from? When my mother met my father on a Californian campus in 1983, they stood under a tree which bore fruit foreign to both. My mother brought one home cupped in the palm of her hand, and her mother planted its seed. Together the women shared its flesh. Together the women shared flesh.

Write a paragraph about your family.

At the moment, my family is American.

We are four people, not five.

My father and mother were Vietnamese in 1975.

They are engineers,

they engineered a new life here

in California, where they met.

They have three children,

two girls and one boy.

The eldest daughter is a writer,

the younger daughter works in a hospital.

The younger son has died.

They do not live in the same house.

Soon, they might be Vietnamese or dead.

All of them will be dead.

Cape Disappointment

nausea arrives like showers sweeping the sandbar, toes edged at the jetty

how our bodies move us and how we move our bodies

how do middle-aged orphans fight over their mother's funeral rites

by watching a bruise form where a brother has touched

the unexpected flush of beach strawberries early in the season

Beside

he w
ho shoo
ts the p
hotog
raph
has been here
all along, standin
g there beside us i
n the nick of time
having arrived just a
fter triggering the cl
ock: one solitude sta
nds beside others, ca
pturing this momen
t for posterity, for he
himself, a man nam
ed Son whose son
removed himself
from frames

cutti   ng in
nto th   em a
nd a   ll aro
und   two
cloc   ks ni
ckin   g the
wire   the v
anis   hing
wic   k: qu
ick,   ever
yon   e say

I left
this in

Đổi Mới

A foundation myth holds that Âu Cơ, the princess of the mountain, married a prince of the sea, Lạc Long Quân, and later gave birth to early kings of the Vietnamese people. There are no mentions of daughters; if they existed, we know neither what they did nor what happened to them. The ancient Vietnamese did not have a family system (in the modern sense), as men and women lived together at will, a tendency antithetical to China's success in establishing rule in the region. Eventually, patriarchal wedding rites found their way into the home, a site where, early in the morning, ông ngoại brought gifts of dowry to bà ngoại's family, marking what later became the third of six ceremonies in what was likely a well-suited (read: arranged) coupling. As a child, bà ngoại took pride in overseeing the field workers of her family estate. Ông ngoại was a well-read man who must've been familiar with Marx, though it is unclear if he discussed such topics with his wife. I know she was responsible for going to the market, later taking my mother along with her. How tender a mother's hand at the small of her daughter's back.

Thirty-two years after they kneel before the altar bowing at pictures of the bride's long-dead ancestors, the slender sticks of incense burning in their hands as they bow to their parents, grateful to have been protected up until now, and bow finally to each other as bride and groom, ash gathering on their knees, they find themselves in a hotel room in Saigon, where their daughter wakes up to the sounds of her mother's nightmare. Whether it was a ghost of war or the ghost in the family, I did not know. As I blinked in the well of darkness which seemed to hold us hostage, I thought I saw my brother's back, the ridges of his spine refracting moonlight. This family has no son. On an evening folk music cruise in Huế, we watched four dancers sing and play the gourd lute. One of them seemed to find me as she went through the routine. My gaze followed her in return. She reminded me of me when I was her age. When I was young, I wanted to be just like her.

Squatting in the kitchen of her parents' home, my mother finds herself in Saigon as she found herself every day of her life. Had she not fled with her mother and sisters, they would be here still, like long beans gathered in the same plastic basket, each with their own imperfections. There is a point at which the body, no matter where it grows, grows no differently than in any other place. Rinsing herbs, the body makes the same movements, takes the same steps. As soon as she leaves this home, she is already on her way back to it, though the journey might take longer than she could have imagined. Upon returning, she no longer recognizes the place, nor her reflection in the mirror. Mother, con nói chuyện với mẹ from here, a place where only words có thể đi được. Each time I look into the mirror, I see you with your back turned toward me.

Misinformation

Maps gave me a wrong turn, so I ended up somewhere else, I tell my friend
at a café downtown.

        Outside, a truck slows at the light, white paint leaking
from it like a car door shut against a wedding dress, a torn flag

                thrashing in the wind.

How is the country? she asks. *How could you leave the city?*

    I tell her about canoes face down atop buggies

        how I am writing lines with white space all around

how there's one main road, one park, one candy shop

    how at the pharmacy, a man approached

Gerber formula shaky in his hands:

        Is this okay for an Asian baby?

Đổi Mới

I am strolling with my father through the corridors of Chợ Lớn, eating an egg tart from one of the vendors.

It is my first visit, my father's first since his flight.

* * *

Flying out of X[1]'s mouth, a bite of an egg tart mistaken for a lemon one.

Spitting, the first white man I loved said, "*What* was that?"

* * *

The egg tart, a custard tart, emerged in twentieth-century Canton from trade with Britain. East meets West.

A variant in Macau emerged at the intersection of Cantonese and Portuguese colonizing influences.

* * *

There is a dish originating in Huế made of rice and tapioca flours, steamed in tiny saucers. Sometimes mashed mung bean is placed in the center of the soft white cakes. Bánh bèo.

"Doesn't it look just like a fried egg?" my mother exclaims, stacking our empty dishes like poker chips.

It is her first time back in the country after thirty-seven years away, and she and my father have been spatting all the way up Việt Nam's spine.

* * *

I have been alive for nearly as long as she has been gone, and it has been that long since I left her body. How many eggs remain, eggs I still carry, eggs my mother carried in carrying me along?

For a time. Meaning that time has passed. Time passes.

* * *

Concurrent with time, so many objects, persons, places drift along, passing those who do not move.

You can change drastically even if you stand still.

* * *

It is Thursday in the only pub on the main street of a small town in central Pennsylvania, and my trivia team is tied with an old biker one named The Merkins across the way.

"What is the name of the Japanese egg noodle dish?" the host asks.

As someone filled with knowledge often useless, a dish I know well lights up inside my mind. The Hiroshima variant, I want to say, and our team writes down okonomiyaki. But when the answers are revealed, the host says, "Egg foo yong."

My face goes flat as a~~ pancake~~ an omelet.

* * *

Doi Moi, a restaurant I nearly walk past in DC. "Exploding with rich flavor and vibrant color, *doi moi* embraces the collision of Vietnamese and French culture..."

A Vietnamese street food joint reimagined through the gaze of others, then regurgitated under neon lights into bowls bigger than my face.

There is nothing new about this place, and I would have stopped for a bite had the line not spilled out the door, snaking around the sidewalk patio.

* * *

At Doi Moi, they garnish inverted conical bowls of phở with huge canoe-cut bones.

Put a decorative bone in my bowl and I'll use it as a weapon.

* * *

"Every year, I think you get angrier," the spouse says to me.

* * *

"Where do you want to go?" a middle-aged law professor I met in France asked me, as we ate pork belly buns outside of ChoLon Modern Asian in downtown Denver.

ChoLon because of Chef Lon's "extensive culinary travels across Asia." A menu boasting of "interpretations of traditional dishes found across the Far East."

"We can go anywhere, I'll take you anywhere. Money is no object."

How did I end up here?

* * *

It was the week before I met my spouse, after moving to Denver for my PhD.

"You'll be a *doctor*," my mother sang, giddy at the prospect.

* * *

If you travel far enough east, you end up in the West, then back East again. Directions, like all things relational, depend on where you are, or who's telling you what.

Territorial disputes continue in the South China Sea. Or the Eastern Sea, as Việt Nam calls it.

The Vietnam War, kháng chiến chống Mỹ, a war in a sequence of wars in a place known as Indochina.

Cape Disappointment

my work inspires mother to write poems I will inherit from her

tears on the page denature like egg whites

American Vietnamese daughter, Vietnamese American mother

we perform for our siblings as well as the dead

may the wet season flood a field of orphans so everything might grow

Misinformation

When he was a boy, the man I love who grew up with many sisters
                    drew a picture of his family: a stick
beside three dogs. *I'm an orphan*, he told his third-grade teacher.

How we came together: a man at the edge of a lake, three dogs swimming
        the fog dipping its hem into water.

                        These myths shift imperceptibly each time we recall them.
Stored along the fault lines of memory
            we pick up where we left off, unaware of what has changed.

Đổi Mới

Minute turns in habit accrete to new rhythms, accumulating to what seems the uncollected hum of routine. No one in the family knows when it began. Perhaps the tendency has always been there. As if my intermittent years away interrupted the slow proof of a family acculturating to their bent course. Beside his wife, my father climbs into a small cot permanently installed in the dining room. Through kelp-green curtains, moonlight filters across their bodies— the parts known beneath the bedding, the toe exposed—just as sunlight did decades ago in a jungle in another country. Where a curtain moves, a mango leaf fluttered. Upstairs, neatly folded piles of shirts, pants, and skirts, flattened purses rest upon the bed in their bedroom, their daughter asleep in her room down the hall, the other rooms uninhabited. In the morning, each wakes in the same position they lay down in. Had he not left Vietnam, he would not have found himself in a one-bedroom apartment in California sleeping beside nine siblings. That first week, they ate the flesh of an animal they had never eaten before, before each of them learned the word *lamb*. As they slept, their bodies grew into the future, like raw rice in the well of a bowl absorbing any moisture around it. Atop my parents' unused bed all our dust gathers.

About your family.

Now, my family

    Used to be five

               Vietnamese

They engineer

    Designed new lives

    Had three children

Either   *or*   *died*

One

     Other one

Another one

They never will

Might have to

Never soon

Cape Disappointment

tides withhold as much as they reveal

what is gleaned from film negatives

in lieu of nouns, pronouns, and names: simile

like a tern circling before its dive-plunge, merging bird and shadow with sea

hunger, like mourning, is defined by what neither has

Root Fracture

coming back to look at you at least what's left of you to look at least at
you not you you least is not the point the point is that I do it do it to go
on I go on doing it this encounter with shape-shifting am I the hero or
the monster perhaps I'm both perhaps you're both both dead and alive
alive in death present in the world as particle and particulate and out of
it the end of a life as important as the other end all ends have a way of
going on ongoing ends let me share what I have learned there is no such
thing as silence I can never be never be silent too much moves beneath
my skin even when I keep still I am traveling to catch up traveling to
meet you perhaps I can catch up with you are you traveling to arrive we
can meet in the middle let's meet in the middle you going from nothing
toward something as something I turn to you uncertain how to know it's
you how will you know me no form is the same twice after all what shall
we bring to identify ourselves what shall I bring from this life to yours
how will I know who you are what if the sound of my voice doesn't
register what if I'm wrong what should I do what will you do there's no
contingency plan in grief only maps without points of reference I don't
know the way to you or my afterlife but I know how I can die how will I
die how will you live can we be together again oblivious to all this in the
white space there are infinite number of ways in the white space there's
another me who knows what to do who's never needed any maps she
sings a song and you sing one too she takes your hand and listens to you
tell me again she says and she listens she is listening to you in the white
space where there are so many ways so many versions of ourselves lost we
can start over again again you say and I will show you show you how to
do it what to do no matter what at no point in time can I be who I was
again this form decomposing memory in decay I am trying to build it up
again trying to build it up with what I know if you make it build it with
me let us compose a form together let us override the overarching drive
let us override the archive let the end be the end of the end and we'll start
in the middle again we can do what we want but we have to want it I
want to be with you again but again I've lost my way tell me how to find
it how to know it's you meet me in the middle in the white space we can

Misinformation

I'm an orphan, my brother said, to a couple who owned the small company
where he worked in the years leading up to his suicide.

The same couple, sitting in my parents' living room, two years after he died:
We took him in as one of us, they said. *He was a model worker. When he tried to quit we didn't let him.*

Đổi Mới

Only when the spider's legs rise to tiptoe, her abdomen readying to release silk, does the spider realize that there must be an electric field at work enabling her flight through the atmosphere. Above land and water there is just one sea, and adrift, the world is no longer quite the maze, surely she will land before she hungers for too long. I do not think she concerns herself with belonging. Does it strike her how many things there are that float, fly, or rise midair? Wind, too, can sweep our strands away from their roots, loosening them elsewhere. Alive, no one reunites like we do: one hand grasps another, a voice calls out and is responded to. When I try to sever ties with my family, not much changes. My leg may cut a course across the water, but water fills back in again. Neither of us asked for our lives, mother, so why can't we ask for less.

The world beyond tennis in 1968 found the United States divided by racial unrest and the war. In the warring place, my father entered his teens accustomed to the sound of distant bombs on his daily walks to school, where he spoke the language of a recent colonizer, where nuns punished his palms with sticks. *Tennis*, from Old French for hold! receive! and take!, all words familiar to those who advance without permission, but in this game there are rules, and pray that the arbiters favor your side. Along with her occupiers, tennis migrated to Vietnam, where only the most privileged held a racket. It is not likely my father picked up the game in Saigon, but perhaps he glimpsed the lizard-green courts from across a street where he would have been shot for walking. The same street we walk, twenty-six years later, my father moving slowly as if unsure of the year. He doesn't speak much, but knows the strings of his racket as well as his own children, mending them as they break. It was his marriage that broke him, not the war, not even the loss of a son which will have happened decades later. Is the fork not an instrument held before a child's mouth, both of them quiet as father feeds son? No, Sơn, not quiet, look at his hands: they're humming.

Misinformation

Your brother is lost, my mother says, *because we didn't believe him.*

He told us there was loud humming inside the walls—Go to sleep, *we said. And he couldn't*

couldn't go to sleep.

Yesterday, your father and I found dead bees inside the attic. Thousands.

Once, when he was still alive, I found a dead bee on the windowsill of our bathroom.

Not thinking much of it

I swept it into the trash with my palm, a motion captured in the dust like afterimage.

The next morning: a dead bee on the windowsill
the other still in the bin.
I told no one.

Omnidirectional

hello my name is

question

don't say anything

my daughter

we didn't know why

because

the smell

no line for hot dogs

C-124

just the money

somebody to sponsor

particularly mother

to kill time

American soldier

just imagine

we know for sure

after Myung Mi Kim

forget everything

son

all camp cry

can you imagine

April 27, 1975

already chaos

I am your father

checkpoint two

sit low

took us to US of A

no communication

Wake Island

find a place to stay

father cry too

everyone on the floor

I worry too much

Son Huu Nguyen transcript

Tug

in a game of tug-of-war two teams pull opposing ends of a rope a vibrational line not any pull but a pull to pull a boat a boat to tow to shore to tow a line two sets of toes on either side their toes in the grass like notes stamped among lines of sheet music this song sliding off scale in lieu of rope my uncles clutch hands pulling brother to brother to brother to brother in a field somewhere i

somewhere i	n Vietnam yea
rs before A	merica interve
nes encircle	d around each
brother's wai	st my mother a
nd her sister	hold onto each
warring brot	her linked this
family chain	threatens to co
me apart but	they are childr
en and this i	s a game childr
en learn to p	lay to test their
strength wit	h each other ag
ainst each ot	her in friendly
contest han	d in hand com
bat clasped a	t her brother's
back my mo	ther can't see
ahead but k	nows what to

do she's three maybe four can't yet know she knows the war can't yet know the years it will take to reunite with her brothers the squall the boat in the fishing vessel lined with sisters she will have known the weight of a rifle as it slips from her arms like rope slipping under into water none of them know how the body readies itself but when the time came they knew what to do

Beside

what
is a fath
er what i
s a fath
er to d
o so far
from his moth
erland now, her sea
rains and fire; he follo
ws his mother onto the
embassy ... his siblin
gs follo... like a sma
ll village... to cere
mony; ... have not
yet died ... this colony   for
is ...   decades
... ...   unreme
bread ...   mber
se ...   ed d
; how many ...   reams, time
... ...   not moving, th
... ...   en she retraced
... ...   his steps, stum
... ...   bling across
... ...   his dead bo
... ...   dy; one clo
... ...   ck ends an
... ...   other begin
... no longer   s again: h
... ...   ere she
... ...   lives, s
... ...   he wh
... ...   o's no
... ...   w dea
ing   them   d to him

this is
not abou
t my moth
er, this is a
bout tw
o mothers:
one miscarries,
suffering alone he
r body bodiless bo
dy, her sister dies in
childbirth poisoned
y amniotic fluid; w
ts to live, who
es who brea
ks down the
barrier; the
medical t
erm for i
njury is t
rauma, t
hat stre
ss the ev
ent of th
e body, h
ow does s
he bear it:
her so
n his
dead
body

what
is a fath
er what i
s a fath
er to d
o so far
from his moth
erland now, her sea
rains and fire; he follo
ws his mother onto the
embassy plane his siblin
gs follow after like a sma
ll village en route to cere
mony; the bees have not
yet died but this colony
is collapsing under
empire, death an u
nchecked umpir
e calling every s
hot; how tende
rly his hands h
old his daughte
r how constant
the small spoo
n held at the m
outh of his son,
a boy w   ho gre
w to rag   e just l
ike his m   other,
the coy b   ride wh
o with hi   m feare
d the frid   ge, fea
ring their   son w
as p   oison
ing   them

this is
not abou
t my moth
er, this is a
bout tw
o mothers:
one miscarries,
suffering alone he
r body bodiless bo
dy, her sister dies in
childbirth poisoned
b   y amniotic fluid; w
ho ge   ts to live, who
di   es who brea
ks down the
barrier; the
medical t
erm for i
njury is t
rauma, t
hat stre
ss the ev
ent of th
e body, h
ow does s
he bear it:
her so
n his
dead
body

with
hands o
f her fat
her, the
hard
mind of her m
other she does not
break will not expo
se herself to others
; how many years
it has taken me
to give myself t
o another; we k
now how fast
flesh separate
s from bone, h
ow suddenly th
e night or dese
rt can no longer
exist; she does n
ot want to believ
e the images th
at crop up, no,
not   at a
ll,   no

for
decades
unreme
mber
ed d
reams, time
not moving, th
en she retraced
his steps, stum
bling across
his dead bo
dy; one clo
ck ends an
other begin
s again: h
ere she
lives, s
he wh
o's no
w dea
d to him

for
decades
unreme
mber
ed d
reams, time
not moving, th
en she retraced
his steps, stum
bling across
his dead bo
dy; one clo
ck ends an
other begin
s again: h
ere she
lives, s
he wh
o's no
w dea
d to him

Đổi Mới

From the beginning, my mother warned me against "puppy love." Then she warned against the affections of white men.

"In college, I had a mathematics professor . . ." she begins.

* * *

When talking about white people, my parents use the phrase "Người Mỹ," or "American." If the American is Black, then "Người Mỹ da đen," so as to color inside the imagination. For everyone else, the words chosen are those which indicate where someone's racial origins reside, even if the person is like them, an American.

"I don't rent to white people," my mother says.

"But what about the tenants in the Cherry house?" I ask.

"They are French," she replies. "Very good people."

* * *

Let me tell you about the French. When they decided to expand their empire, they destroyed a citadel in Gia Định, reducing the city's population by 80 percent.

After wresting control, the French used enslaved people and convict labor to fuel a building spree in the area which came to be known as Sài Gòn.

When you are on a spree, you are unrestrained and nothing yet has stopped you.

* * *

Set in French Indochina, Marguerite Duras's novel *The Lover* follows the clandestine romance of a French adolescent of unfortunate financial circumstances and an older Chinese business magnate.

A scene from the film adaptation: amid a spree of afternoons fucking, the nude girl languidly drags her body down a few short steps, lengthening the distance from her lover.

* * *

We don't talk explicitly enough about power and money in relationships.

I don't know how to separate power and money from love, so I am choosing to separate myself from my mother.

Each day I choose again to remain separated, and it is hard, because despite everything, I _____ her.

Fuck filial piety, I tell my therapist, and every week we talk about my desire to reach out to my parents.

I can't. I won't. I shouldn't.

* * *

"If you talk or write about our family, we will be forced to take action," my mother said the last time we spoke. I knew what she meant by "take action," since she had previously threatened to sue for slander.

Truth, like a directional, is relative.

* * *

Let me tell you about my mother.

Đổi Mới

She watches mainly WWII films, attentive like a sentry, retracing the steps of someone trying to find her way out. Her aging mother sits quietly before her in what my mother refers to as "any day now." Bà ngoại had asked to be closer to her daughters in Southern California. In the early months of postwar Vietnam, my mother pleaded for them to flee and so the facade of an evening walk, silent, brisk, stopping to recall, paralyzing terror, a frantic hand searching for my mother's to drag her as they moved along half-lit alleys. I am trying to remember the details, but this is not my memory. The state visited indignities upon the women in my bloodline, that state, this state, and she upon her daughters, and so this line now finds enclosure. In the dark we cannot know for sure which liquid emerges from the body, and when I ask why WWII, my mother replies, *Because someone is always running or hiding, and it's black-and-white.*

Her birth, her birthing me, both began with a sentence, one which neither of us will survive. The more we find language, in this one or another, perhaps the clearer it becomes, the inadequacy of any verbal communication. Even an extreme form of parenting, such as matriphagy, involves a touching. And who makes the first offering, the body for biting, or maw for eating? A silent transfer, by which I mean no one speaks, but music gathers as parent and child move toward each other. What other task exists if not biological? Love, however defined, must be to ensure a fitness, so who cares if it's conditional. On my wall I begin to hammer a nail upon which will hang an image of my father, younger than I am now. The vibration of the movement dislodges one of my young mother, and she tumbles out from the glass, the wooden frame fracturing at two joints. It may be easier to replace, but having been taught to avoid waste, I will repair it and hang my child self in her place. I exist to resist the will of another. And so it goes.

Family Portraits

an old expectation
of organisms
           some form of symmetry

fold until there is one
fold
           until enough parts
resemble each other

however duplicate

                  symmetry
is approximate

not all sand dollars are whole

      *

           in a young face
the unfolding
           of an older one

young man
young father
my young grandfather beside

son wife and daughters

each face a part

of the one beside it

                        young ghosts
waiting
        to take their place

        *

center the prized
                son

everyone in the photograph
has
will have

a son

undone comes a poppy

        *

        the frame
borders
a country   reimagined

the way language

approaches something true

who what that
who what that there

        *

                              to revise

           come on in
                     and welcome back

                              *

           where algal cast

           in low tide

                     sheer
           curtains strewn

           ba mẹ's kitchen sink

                              unseen force

           what falls

           unforeseen
                              *

behind the camera

sound
unfurls

distant clock hands

*

anybody
can be

a body

*

surface shells
appear   those

who no longer
go to ground

*

who beside
who behind

        a camera
is survived by what it saw

má says why remember that
ma says nothing

can nothing
stay

    *

orphans now
        who hope
for orphans of their own

naturally

an orphan gives her daughters
her haircut

precaution
    against predation

aesthetic
tradition

    *

peninsula implies

third coast
      place

        where parts converge

diverge
I was born

      facing
Vietnam

two coasts
      too far for crows
      to fly

east to west
west   looking east

alluvium sinks my toes

      *

in tug-of-war
      two sides face off

without rope
use arms

      bring
the other side
closer

all this time watching arms

now I see
             her bandage

there comes a time
when a wound

continues undressed

                    *

a child playing

                  a child playing
dress-up

in her mother's
wedding   áo dài

in the wedding photo
my child's uncertain smile

on her face

                    *

             at night
the mirror

a family reunion

me
mẹ   ma

mà ma

     *

     palin-

ode

war was won
mẹ never went to sea
no son to take his life

I have no child

I've been

     a daughter
inscribing

     in sand

subjunctive dreams

     *

double

       exposure means

       we can be
the same place
twice

       to be an orchestra
of one

one needs
instruments

     and memory

     *

evening falls

          one shore
and another

     decades
the distance
        between

high tide conceals

who emerges
from underground

night
shift moths
                        tripping thru
            coastal mugwort

bà ngoại's hands
                        rinsing her face

            four daughters'

palms lift
            to do the same

                        I wipe

the camera lens
between each

            time lapse

Subjunctive

When the tide returns, who advances, smudging pockmarks off the mudflats.

Off the floor of her bunker, my mother lifts her heels so she might see.

This is as tall as she'll ever be and even in hiding she grows toward light.

Though she cannot see them, she knows how clams nudge deeper under cover. One limb slips out from a crack—

Slipping into sand is like slipping into shadows where running takes the form of waiting.

Many years later, her daughter rewinds the mother's wedding. Rewinds and pauses. Pauses and rewinds, trailing a finger along the wrinkles of the transferred tape.

There you are, when I find the woman I know in a girl I'll never meet.

Rake your hands slowly through the mud until you run into something.

The bride lifts her gloved hand to ward off sun. Buddha help us when we go to war.

Misinformation

I told your grandfather to take my brothers and go, mother says,

                      so they wouldn't get conscripted.

            She would stay and help my grandmother

      with the family business, a pharmacy. One by one, her younger sisters

chose to stay and help my mother, dominoes falling into place.

After he left, the war ended, there was nothing, no pharmacy.

        A woman and five daughters hiding in the dark.

                  Wind swept through

   empty alleys, boarded shops.

             Asked to ask a neighbor for some rice

my mother watched the tanks roll in, boys in uniform razing over the dead

      who had been swept off to one side.

Đổi Mới

The longer they remained hiding by the coast, the sooner no one would know where they were any longer, or if they were. Underground where everything is concealed, bà ngoại and her daughters learned to discern each other's rustlings: an unseen hand lifting black chopsticks, rice against a lip, grain by grain the grain of one sister's whisper disappearing into another. They name each object and each other, mẹ, cơm, đũa, nước, but in such darkness words can stand for so much more: a tether that threads them through to daylight, hands clasped between each body like beads nestled between tight knots. Isn't this how story-telling works, where one dream stops before another starts? Each day takes us further away from who we once were to who we soon will be. Into my dry eye I drop an artificial tear as across a global crisis bà ngoại does the same, though her eyes are now a foggy mirror. She looks away from me as she speaks, and I watch her reflection on the sliding door. Does not our memory furnish the journey of our unfinished existence?

And so generations in a family pass and are like one regenerating organism. Whether schizophrenia manifested in bà cô before the American War or in my cousin in America amid its latest interventions, I can still remember the sound when we were all alive, the echo of cha mẹ's voices down the open halls of the elementary school in summer, my siblings and I shouting out as we pedaled harder to catch up as evening descended in a quiet layer of dust, the hum of all our spokes whirring in the dark, and I haven't forgotten what a body looks like as it cycles so far that I can only make it out by the sounds that travel back to me. All cheerful memories are like a single one, quickly forgotten in times of danger. A photograph can jolt one back to a position the body hasn't worn in decades. In old pictures, a girl whose posture I know as mine, except the year is 1964. Behind her, a portrait of her mother's family, and here I find my brother again. If the escape route is long enough, it leads you back to where it first opened.

Cape Disappointment

sedge and sea asparagus submerge, reemerge

what happens when the time comes and the tide doesn't

startled, my mother and I find each other in passing

the robin with mouths to feed reverses just before my window

it isn't you, mother, looking me in the eye before you strike

////

Cape Disappointment

open the window to erase your ghost or maybe let one in

I unlatch like a cello case, air filling every dent in the velvet

a burr in the wool sock, that's what inspired Velcro

why does this avocado rot before it can ripen

time and time again it is time we can't apprehend

Misinformation

Out in Texas Hill Country I am squatting over a kiddie pool
filled with ice, noodling for beer.

The birthday boy mans a roiling crawdad pot
his five-year-old loading clay pigeons into the trap.

As the eyes of rifles trace and fire

kids rumble around the fields
in dirt bikes without helmets.

In the dust, a woman calls out to her black dog
using a racial epithet.

Like a bird loaded into a trap, I am frozen in place, hoping no one sees me.

But everything goes on just the same:

shirtless men teach me horseshoes, gently
a wife stores cheesecake in the fridge for later.

I pee a little in my boots when we take shots after sundown
because I am jumping, jumpy.

A Black neighbor joins late, everybody's
glad to see him.   *Hey, Frank!* they say.

The dog comes over to check out the stranger
and they sweetly greet each other.

What's your name, boy? the man asks.

Frank, a woman replies.

Đổi Mới

When we found small tins tucked in unused drawers and unnoticed parts of the fridge, we fingered the language we would later recognize as his second, the one ông bà nội nudged him toward because he was their eldest, and shouldn't the eldest integrate with the whites of that time? Within a month upon arrival, my father and his brother enrolled in engineering courses at Pasadena City College, taking shifts as attendants in the school parking lot. As his heavy eyelids lowered on their evening bus ride, shadows of palm trees washing over his face, did he think for a moment that he was back home? In California the palm provides neither shade nor sustenance; this tree is ornamental, but we know what happens when naphthenic and palmitic acids are dropped on it. *Beurre*, I tried to read, suspicious of the tin's greasy substance. I did not think to taste it, fearing bitterness, or worse, what if it burned me? Both child and refugee learn the words that surround them as well as words that mean harm. With the palm of his hand a father may soothe or signal, but what about the palm that holds a child down gently so that a mother may strike?

Of the loneliest creature on earth, it is said to be neither a blue nor fin whale but a whale singing at a frequency higher than either, and low on the range of what the human ear detects as a bass note, lonely because no other whale has responded to it, lonely because we want to believe that we alone can hear it, we who have never found it. Sometimes, when you describe another you are describing yourself, the mirror refracting a photograph of just last night, thousands of miles away, a moment moving further away from you, no matter how often you return to it. Isn't this what home is, you holding the photograph, the photograph holding you? In it, you see the faces of your grandparents in your parents', and in your face your parents see their own. Bà ngoại sits beside the fiddle-leaf fig, your sister at her side. Multiple generations, each aging in the same direction. Between them, a tree where a brother should be. Sometimes, to love your family you have to become a stranger, dead or alive.

After a child mất, a mother remains a mother, a father, a father, who we are depends on who we are to each other, even if we cannot see each other anymore. As a child, I learned via mimicry, as insects and plants do, in order to survive. They worried about money, I worried about money. If a word was uttered in a state of anger, I uttered the same word when I became angry, connecting a sound to a feeling, ignorant of the history of that sound. And so I learned the dialect of my parents, learning over thirty years later what this dialect revealed about their xenophobia. Despite carefully plotted trails and walkways, there remain paths worn into the ground, "paths of desire" which may offer a more direct route between destinations. A military aircraft full of refugees flies as the crow does, but neither's a straight path. A fishing vessel, lined with sisters who will become my mother and aunts, teeters through a squall, and lands in Malaysia before they all land in California. For those who flee, paths of desire are ones of necessity: my parents left their country, taking their lives into their hands. If I can take my own life, then I can take my life with me. Con thương cha mẹ, but I didn't ask to be born, so I don't owe you a thing.

Root Fracture

open
tice pa
logic
d it is th ing th
ne then you're on the ri
one wa back any we can go off trac
llow along with your finger where you'
el you go in you come out but so much el
ating of filtering out about your story let me
keep my mouth shut to let you in let you
ht if you want it I want it too I want you to
rcumstances under which under which we ar
ash a sound it falls somewhere between t
umble then perhaps a crack did you hea
here you are could you feel what we feel
it can go forward and back overlap loop
ack three steps forward two steps back a
their own moving walkway one ran with i
hi s we can't take back would u tal
if metimes I wrestle wit my dy I
tro to

of various rituals and repetitions here is one way to know that you are dead this is the way to kr
you do it right then you did it right no quandary about it open a book any book you can fin
you find one can you find it sometimes patience takes practice patience takes patience all of v
needs developing in the afterlife listen to me listen in chronological order it may not work othe
open a book are there words can you read it is there anything there to read put your finger t
page as if tracing words tracing lines if none then good you're on the right track a track implie
ways of going one way forward one way back anytime we can go off track put your finger to the
read a story to the blankness follow along with your finger where you've been they say birth
entrance and death a lit tunnel you go in you come out but so much else can enter and be le
many are the ways of infiltrating of filtering out about your story let me hear it let's hear it I'll
open all my windows I'll keep my mouth shut to let you in let you out you can come a
however whenever you want if you want it I want it too I want you to stay a little longer I c
avoid thinking about the circumstances under which under which we are talking can we talk a
talking a little longer I unleash a sound it falls somewhere between the music and the rocks bet
the music and the rocks a rumble then perhaps a crack did you hear the earth quake before yo
it could you feel it from where you are could you feel what we feel can you feel the music it so
forth when set in motion it can go forward and back overlap loop over on itself I take three
forward then two steps back three steps forward two steps back at the airport I watch two s
running each running on their own moving walkway one ran with it one ran back it took her l
but she made it back some things we can't take back would you take it back if you could woul
take back your body give it life sometimes I wrestle with my body I want to throw myself out a
myself I am against myself I want to tear to chew to shove everything out to empty the bo
empty it out how sound will travel then without obstruction no complications it moves th
then beyond I want to hear your story about your story let me hear it let it in let it open me be

Tug

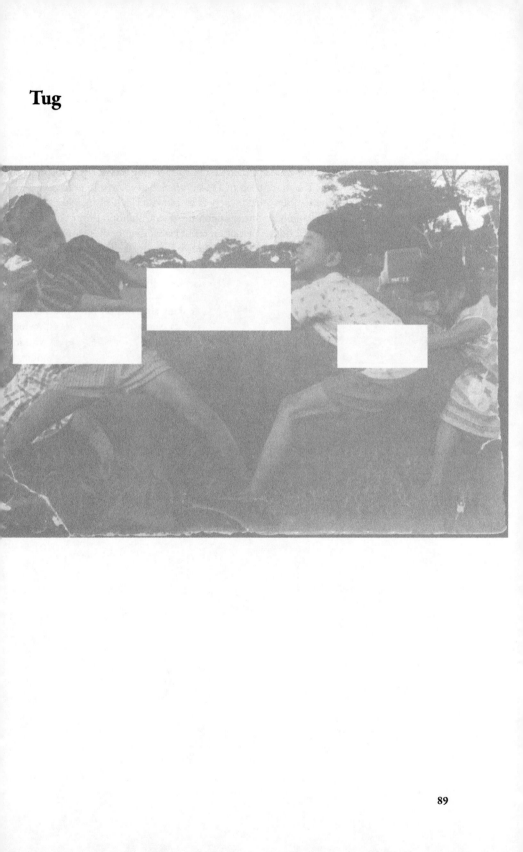

of a photograph Barthes's studium tells what has happened as it was happening this one split second back i
I travel back in time to return to a place I've never been to a place which had to exist in order to exist on
my mind now do I see the moment the stadium a field where grass grows far past my mother's young an
rear of an automobile parked beside the boundary of trees upon my own childhood thirty years later can
this terrain the grass the open field children's bodies in motion testing what their bodies are made of becau
can because it feels good to do so to strive in this way four bodies two brothers facing off a sister each at th
these are the facts of the photograph the striped shorts plaid smock variations on the noses of my grandp
hair pulled back hair let down know   uncles these two brothers I am both su
and not surprised to see them as th   s to say the same the same bodies the
which here would seem foreign to th   aking after surgery finds that part of he
which u   s its conto   previously
not hav   e the smooth stretches bumps small cr   working
moveme   a stranger as if her dead body in photo   bodies de
people very much alive as I know them now and yesterday and evidence of who will die but now here
photograph and present moment they exist but what strikes me is how they hold each other which is a
which they hold themselves together securely so that the grasp does not come loose four hands in contest
two knots to embrace is also secure which also keeps another's body in place in time for the time bein
somebody lets go or breaks free is the love of a sibling pure until somebody realizes they hadn't been able
things all too clearly and so the fog of the family lifts but just for a moment because when your country is
you do not have time to consider how to love your brothers cautiously because it's black-and-white isn't
photograph the war the decision to keep on living even though you couldn't say why or what for I cannot
for my mother or her brothers or that which had happened that which will have happened by the tim
uncover this photograph in the country where I was born where they are parents of children whom they
against each other in proxy competition here where I belong I long to hold my hands around my brother's

Beside

I kept
as still a
s I cou
ld, a
lways lookin
g for a way o
ut; all I can s
ay is what
happene
d: with,
and the
n with
out—
witho
ut wor
ds I h
ave no
thing,
nothin
g I
can
sa
y

the lo
ve of my
life, she
wrot
e to nobody,
no one, not eve
n to herself; befo
re the camera sh
e smiling using
finger as a k
nife; the len
ths she'll go
to get them
to straight
en to get a
er children
to listen; i
ow it is a b
attle a war
when she h
as done wh
at she has to
do: it is emp
tiness inside
that holds w
hat she wants

I left
this in

he w
ho shoo
ts the p
hotog
raph
has been here
all along, standin
g there beside us i
n the nick of time
having arrived just a
fter triggering the cl
ock: one solitude sta
nds beside others, ca
pturing this momen
t for posterity, for he
himself, a man nam
ed ... son whose son
removed himself
from frames
cutti ng in
to th em a
ll aro
, two
oc ks ni
kin g the
ire the v
wanis hing
k: qu
ever
e say

Đổi Mới

So now something instilled in her since she was young, especially these years after her child took his life, becomes undeniably false: if your child goes off the path set for him by his parents, a path set in motion by the parents of his parents, and their parents, and so on, what happens eventually is the child is ruined or returns to a poverty of your ancestors. She imagines her dead son is happier, as her daughter does, though neither would admit to kin thinking. She toiled so that she would not have to suffer, though the toiling brought on newer forms of suffering. When I tell my mother about a mother who believes that the yellow moth which fluttered into the kitchen, confused above the steaming pots, was her dead son, my mother responds, Your brother is not a moth, but the space through which the moth found its way inside. Then she tells me about her plans to install paver in the yard. Only when I realize that any stone can comprise a gravestone do I understand that the garden is also a cemetery. What of me begins to rot, and what will burst right through it?

One morning, for the sake of my daughter's life, I cut myself out of my mother's life. Eventually there comes a point when the price you pay for being a child continues to grow, and the debt becomes so vast that even your death won't settle the tab. So you cut your losses and start again elsewhere. Except the family is a tapestry of fine threads inextricably woven; you cut one and it's still hanging there, tethered to all other fibers, minus one. I don't have a daughter, and because my mother is one, I don't know if I will. I don't have a son, and because my brother was one, I don't know if I will. As in a crowded garden, I want to keep father, mother, and child separate from each other, so that they might each grow at their own pace. Even gaps in a fabric become a pattern to strive for, offering space for fiber tension to flow. When my mother released her aging mother from her care, I imagined that bà ngoại embraced the wound her daughter opened as if embracing my mother as a newborn. In a time of war, I learned, you can get rid of your life with a rifle, or prolong the act until the endgame.

Each of us describes my brother's death in different terms, though the fact of his absence interrupts us indiscriminately. Do we know how he found his life, if from inside it looked like a cage shaped exactly like his body, except two sizes too big, growing as he grew, condensing when he made himself small, and no matter what he did, he couldn't dissolve its borders, not even while he slept. I don't think it let him sleep. At night, fighting sleep, I stay up as if hoping I'll catch wind of something. Tonight, or years ago, a wolf chased a deer past the cabin's front door and out onto lake ice, where fate met each discriminately. Borders dissolved, but which one, between predator and prey, or stage and props? Anywhere there is a hole there are traces of arrival and departure. The wind becomes a palimpsest of the creature no longer here, and a song—or is it a cry?—emerging from nowhere, on its way to nowhere, passes through until the textures of the earth absorb it entirely. Sound: a body's way of making itself known. Silence: a way of knowing.

/////

Root Fracture

in one version of the story you're alive you wake up you'd been trying for years to get it back for so long that you can't remember what it is or was anymore you knew you'd been trying you couldn't leave and then one day your things were gone all that remained was an empty bed frame like a cage broken down and left open like a trap ajar by all accounts you were free you had cut yourself off you cut us off and we we rejoiced it was a sign mother said if you could leave then you were well enough to well enough to go no one asked where or how or when only the fact of it remained we celebrated you grown and flown where did you go in this version of the story before you're alive and wake up I imagine you sitting on the side of your bed in the room of a house of a man you knew briefly from nights playing badminton perhaps all that volleying turned into small parcels of belonging did your heart swell in recognition of it were you seen as you hadn't been I've been seeing you now seeing you leap to hit that birdie your dark head in a court of other dark heads all eyes darting to follow to catch so as to strike striking a letting go of the bird it lets it go over to the other side and often it comes back over and back how I find pleasure in sending the bird between us over and back that is not an efficient way of winning of ending the match I know but oh how I never play to win I never win I wanted the volley to continue never to stop in this version of the story you're alive picky as ever staring at your chicken sandwich while I lie by the window in another country watching clouds skip like stones along the lake as long as the world moves along I can stay this delirium in which the sparkling tailed hummingbird zips to feed from petals just beside me I move and he is gone and the rain again in the rain I recreate what I saw try to conjure him and he's back I try to conjure and he's back why conjure then at all but to listen for his arrival in the hum of his departure in this story you're back you lose all patience volleying birdies with me but I can't help it I don't want the bird to touch the ground in this story a bee crawled out of the kitchen what had she been doing when I could not see her I lifted her up and let her go do you think she'll make it I ask but you don't hear me yet you don't hear me you don't hear the bee her

Cape Disappointment

what might distinguish museum from mausoleum

objects which don't reproduce

my portrait reveals the furrow my mother carries which her mother carried

no need for lighthouses placed close together

a reflection on water as on glass aren't they ghosts

Misinformation

Let me be frank.

At readings in front of strangers and friends, I tell the story
about bees
but each time the words are different.

The hum of each crowd, different.

We are here with each other and there's so much we do not say.

At my brother's funeral
I didn't hold my mother's hand, I held my brother's hand.
I didn't hold my brother's hand

no one held my hand.

Đổi Mới

There arrives a time when neither mother nor father knows more about a child than the child could know about herself: when she has been gone longer than the time it took to form her first memory. Perhaps one day my mother will tell me what she knows and can't yet forget. Perhaps one day my father will tell me that he doesn't know why he stood by as she raged, and I will tell him how I saw his sorrow, even when he looked away. When a father helps his daughter to skate, they both hold hands, though she is moving away from him. With the same hands I used to keep balance, I now am writing my way back home. Even biologists now move away from the perspective of an individual to focus on cooperation and interconnectivity. In the old-growth forest, as in the family, of course there is conflict. But also negotiation, and forms of reciprocity so singular to the one who offers it that I think of it as the song one sings while moving alone in the wild. Anywhere there is life on land, there are webs underground passing nourishment, signal, and water. No tree in nature clears a space, setting out to find its own way. It is only a person who thinks to do this. All this time I have been moving in the wrong direction.

When I was a child, my father would hide in the dark to jump out when we least expected it, and precisely because we loved him so much, we looked away from him as he looked away from his wife who had temporarily metamorphosed into a different kind of mother. Looking back now, I see each of us looking in the wrong place. It is easier for a child to focus on one monster, because to know that there are multiple, in varying degrees and numerous places, can be too much to bear for one so small. And how to comprehend an intermittent one? The days we spend estranged gather like snow dusting on the needles of a fir tree. Eventually the load will tip over, as ice calves from glaciers, but the calving of ice is not the same as the calving of a whale or wildebeest. There comes a time for separation, and let us hope it is neither too early nor too late. Nothing split fits back the same, but I don't want things the way they were. Perhaps a single moment of light in the family could reveal the past to have been illusion. Kintsugi, the art of putting pieces back together but lining the cracks in gold so as to illuminate what once was broken.

Root Fracture

e

e

if w
e acce
pt the c
amera's r
ecord let
it be kn
own how
she staged eac
h of us every g
esture, we could
n't say no: phot
ographs trigger
ones not take
n, pictures f
orgotten in
our minds—
she cannot re
member what
she has done,
what did she do
to destroy such
wretched daught
ers, before h
er death she
stands on the
se steps, a m
udden child:
what holds
many of us
let her hind
undone to h
er, to all of u
s the war, ho
w it fores
hadows

105

if w
e acce
pt the c
amera's r
ecord let
it be kn
own how
she staged eac
h of us every g
esture, we could
n't say no: phot
ographs trigger
ones not take
n, pictures f
orgotten in

w it cuts
hadows

                              if w
                            e acce
                           pt the c
                          amera's r
                          ecord let
                           it be kn
                          own how
          e   she staged eac
                        h of us every g
                        esture, we could
                        n't say no: phot
                        ographs trigger
                        ones not take
                        n, pictures f
                        orgotten in
                        our minds—
                        she cannot re
                        member what
                        she has done,
          e   *what did she do*
                     to deserve such
                     wretched childr
                     en; she kno
                        ws now she
                        wasn't me
                        ant for thi
                        s, didn't m
                        ean to do i
                        t any of it:
                        let her und
                        o it, let it be
                        undone to h
                        er, to all of u
                        s: the war, ho
                        w it fores
                   hadows

if w
e acce
pt the c
amera's r
ecord let
it be kn
own how
she staged eac
h of us every g
esture, we could
n't say no: phot
ographs trigger
ones not take
n, pictures f
orgotten in
our minds—
she cannot re
member what
she has done,
what did she do
to deserve such
wretched childr
en; she kno
ws now she
wasn't me
ant for thi
s, didn't m
ean to do i
t any of it:
let her und
o it, let it be
undone to h
er, to all of u
s: the war, ho
w it fores
hadows

Đổi Mới

Why did you do this? Why did you do this? said bà nội to my brother at the edge of his rented coffin. Was she wrong to center agency amid such self-contained violence, when after all, hadn't we been taught to clean up after ourselves, sweeping clear our tracks as we go. Tasked with closing his accounts, I found each of them empty or squared away months in advance by one who no longer advances except as a memory passed back and forth, he moving past us. Three times does her palm pass across the kitchen counter, my mother sweeping ash from his altar, huddled grains in a small bowl anchoring red incense sticks. Some sticks are bright, some have faded, and gathered in one place, they reveal how much time has elapsed. Even now, as in the past, we reuse a vessel, big or small. Raw rice, like cremains, should be stored in a dark, enclosed space lest they absorb respiration. *Mẹ ơi*, said my father as he hoisted his mother out of her wheelchair, from one torn country to another, where in the other room, his younger brother struggles to breathe, wrestling the virus nestled in each of them. It doesn't matter where we go; where there is time, there we will die.

Beneath a sunburnt lawn, long-gone remnants of the pepper tree two refugees planted as they built their home from the ground up, preparing for the arrival of their first and only son as two young girls played in a cardboard box nearby, where above there thrives an olive tree, as evergreen and tolerant of the Californian drought as its predecessor. These species have been introduced, meaning each are native elsewhere. Regardless of species, fungal threads link nearly every plant via subterranean circuitries. News, need, and supply pass from tree to tree where it is understood that the health of the whole hinges upon that of each neighbor; dying trees offer up their stores to those who still can use them. What connects those living within wooden boxes constructed along the cul-de-sac above? Perhaps the sounds which enter us unregistered, the cry I swallowed dragging sharps across my flesh while down the hallway my still-alive brother wondered if the humming in the walls was real. It has been years since the state's last major earthquake and still the aftershocks arrive.

At first no one in the family notices anything because time in a house acts very much like a frozen stream in spring: everything melts, albeit not uniformly, and so there are bits cut off from the body that once was whole, and trapped in the rocks and root work, some ice fragments melt later than others. It is only a matter of time before reentry, but when I left home I did not think I would come back. In departure and return we recognize the difference in each other, detect what absence has now made foreign. Thirty-seven years after fleeing Vietnam, my mother shields her body with my father's as I trail behind them on a street in Ho Chi Minh City. Here, chỉ có xe đạp, she whispers, where now motorbikes move as if in murmuration, spilling around us as we cross. In the wounded daughter a recognition of the wounded mother, a way of understanding where we are, even if divided. A storm can disperse seeds due to high altitudes, as war displaces parts to a whole. Between parent and child, coiled strands that sequence and distinguish their beings. I think of my mother's hair, braided or unraveled, how it grows even as she cuts it.

he w
ho shoo
ts the p
hotog
raph
has been here
all along, standin
g there beside us i
n the nick of time
having arrived just a
fter triggering the cl
ock: one solitude sta
nds beside others, ca
pturing this momen
t for posterity, for he
himself, a man nam
ed Son whose son
removed himself
from frames
cutti   ng in
to th   em a
nd a   ll aro
und   , two
cloc   ks ni
ckin   g the
wire   the v
anis   hing
wic   k: qu
ick,   ever
yon   e say

Acknowledgments

With deep gratitude for—

Emma Paterson, who found and believed in my work before I knew how to do so. I remain in awe of you.

Chris Richards and the magnificent team at Scribner.

Willapa Bay AiR, the Randolph College Low-Residency MFA family, the Helene Wurlitzer Foundation, the National Endowment for the Arts, Brown University's American Studies department, and the University of Tennessee at Knoxville for the gift of time, space, and community support. To the University of Pittsburgh for their support in a fledging Vietnamese diaspora dialogue project.

My fellow companions in the grueling 15/15: Chet'la Sebree, E.C. Belli, R. Eric Raymond, Lilly Lam, Ashley Dailey, Benjamin Grimes. These words and images exist because of our exchanges—thank you for the shared space of friendship, encouragement, and epistles.

Richard Greenfield, Jane Wong, Cindy Juyoung Ok, S. Brook Corfman, Dawn Lundy Martin, Angie Cruz, and Yona Harvey. For your belief in me as a human and literary person—your work on and off the page inspires me daily.

Those pollinators at the University of Denver: Bin Ramke, Selah Saterstrom, W. Scott Howard. Thank you for opening my mind to the quiet and intricate music of multiple realms.

Mentors passed, past, and present: Lucie Brock-Broido, Cal Bedient. I wouldn't be here without you.

She Who Has No Master(s), especially: Dao Strom, Hoa Nguyen, Lily Hoang, and Vi Khi Nao for showing me how powerful and fierce collaboration can be, and that both Vietnamese kith and the Vietnamese language can be radically tender.

Love and support from the Nguyen and Finan families. In loving memory of Oliver Khoi Nguyen, ông bà ngoại, ông nội, and George Finan. I envision your spectral selves as young ghosts in joint laughter and wonder.

The gift of hope and daily celebrations: Benjamin, Peregrine Sông, Beckett, and Daisy. Max, may you forever leap across fern-filled ravines and swim gracefully inside alpine lakes. In all of our hearts, the meadow is abloom.

Notes

In recognition of influences and inspirations:

All altered photographs are familial. The family portraits where one member is missing are ones where my brother Oliver cut himself out—two years before taking his life in 2014.

The prose blocks in "Đổi Mới" owe syntactical debt to Jenny Erpenbeck's *Visitation* (translated from the German by Susan Bernofsky).

"Notes on the Fractures" takes after Robert Hass's "Notes on 'Layover'" from *Sun Under Wood*, and the concept that revision can be a form of addition from a workshop with Monica Youn at the Kundiman Retreat in 2019.

"Again" owes the debt of plot recursion to Melisa Tien's play, *Best Life*.

"Omnidirectional" is intended to be read in any direction, with repetition and omission of any fragment; it is indebted to Myung Mi Kim's "[accumulation of land]" from *Penury* and Kim's own audio reading of the poem on the Poetry Foundation website.